Arista

Grade 2

awake

or asleep

AWAKE OR ASLEEP

written by Alix Shulman / designed and illustrated by Frank Bozzo

Young Scott Books

Printed in U.S.A. All Rights Reserved.

Text © 1971 by Alix Shulman.

Illustrations © 1971 by Frank Bozzo.

Published by Young Scott Books, a Division of
Addison-Wesley Publishing Co., Inc., Reading, Mass. 01867.

Library of Congress Catalog Card No. 72-141665.

SBN: 201-09106-2.

to D.D. and S.S.

One morning
Sally woke up wondering
if she were really awake.

At night
she always dreamed
she was awake
when she was really
sound asleep.

This morning she thought,
"Maybe I'm asleep
and only dreaming I'm awake."

But when she saw her brother Daniel
racing to the kitchen ahead of her,
Sally leaped out of bed
just as though she were awake

and forgot to wonder whether she really was or not.

Not until she got
a knot in her shoelace
did she remember
that she might be asleep after all
and only dreaming
that she had a knot in her shoelace.

The more she wondered
the less certain she felt.

If she really were awake,
wouldn't she know it?
And here she was not knowing it . . .

or not knowing if she knew it . . .

or not knowing
if she knew if she knew it . . .

or not knowing
if she knew if she knew if she knew it.

"I'm stuck!"
said Sally, giving a hard tug on the knot.
For whether the knot was real or not,
she would have to unknot it
to get her shoe on,
awake or asleep.

Out came the knot.

Sally ran to the kitchen.

"How can I tell if I am awake or asleep?"
Sally asked Daniel.

"Pinch yourself and see if it hurts."

"Of course it will hurt if I pinch myself," Sally thought.

"I've dreamed of being hurt by bears and brothers.
Couldn't I dream of being hurt by pinches?"

But just to make sure, she pinched herself.

It hurt.

"OUCH!"
shouted Sally,
awake or asleep.

"How can I tell if I'm awake or asleep?"
Sally asked her father.

"If you were asleep,"
laughed her father,
"you wouldn't be in the kitchen
asking silly questions.
Do you want cinnamon or jam
on your toast?"

In her dreams Sally often sat in the kitchen
eating silly meals, like worms
or bears
or brothers.

Then why couldn't she,
in a dream,
be in the kitchen
asking silly questions?

"Marmalade," she said,
and reached for her orange juice.

Suddenly in the glass
she saw her own face
staring up at herself
looking down at her face . . .

staring up at herself
looking down at her face.

"I am dreaming," she thought.
"I must be dreaming to get stuck
staring at my own face
during breakfast!"

"Sally,
  you're daydreaming again,"
  said her mother.
"Please drink your orange juice
  before your toast gets cold."

"Mom,"
  Sally asked,
"how do you know if I am awake or asleep?"

Her mother laughed.
"With you, Sally, I don't know.
I just guess."

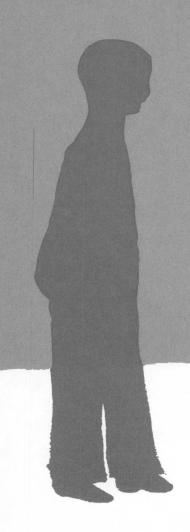

"Race you to school," Daniel called.

And suddenly

it didn't matter if she were awake or dreaming . . .

She only wanted to get to school first,

awake or asleep.

Author

Alix Shulman is a native of Cleveland and took her B.A. at Western Reserve. A childhood interest in philosophy and metaphysics led her to post-graduate study in philosophy and later in mathematics at N.Y.U. She is an active feminist, presently involved in assessing the prejudices in children's media.

All her varying interests have converged in her writing for children—a book concerned with mathematical concepts, a biography of Emma Goldman as well as the philosophical probings of this book. She lives in New York City with her husband and two children.

Artist

Frank Bozzo thinks he may have become an artist because he sat in the back of a very large classroom in the Bronx. Big though it was, someone must have known what he was doing back there because he kept being asked to do stage sets, school murals, and holiday decorations. Vaguely expecting to be an essayist or waiter or something, he kept having art jobs until gradually he was a confirmed and sometimes-satisfied artist.

By now he has illustrated five children's books and countless record covers, annual reports, magazine commissions and done paintings. He lives with his wife and young daughter in New York City and teaches at the School of Visual Arts where he is careful never to know what goes on in the back of the room.